NR9

A CASE OF SAMPLES

A CASE OF SAMPLES

Poems 1946—1956

by

KINGSLEY AMIS

LONDON
VICTOR GOLLANCZ LTD
1957

First published November 1956
Second impression April 1957

PRINTED IN GREAT BRITAIN
BY BUTLER AND TANNER LTD,
FROME AND LONDON

TO MY MOTHER AND FATHER

CONTENTS

A CASE OF SAMPLES

BED AND BREAKFAST

Sometimes a parting leaves only a room
That frames a void in yellow wallpapers,
Unpersoned by such brief indifferent use;
But love, once broken off, builds a response
In the final turning pause that sees nothing
Is left, and grieves though nothing happened here.

So, stranger, when you come here to unpack,
To look like me excited on the garden,
Expect from me nothing but a false wish
That, going, you ignore all other partings,
And find no ghosts that growl or whinny of
Kisses from nowhere, negligible tears.

LEGENDS

Sleepy, the nurse forgot the end of the story,
And offered a plausible mystery instead;
So the young rider, weakened by age she added,
Lost his message and went astray for good,
Turning off the highroad of history
To wander endlessly in fabled night.
Deceived like this, children in their dreams
Set food before the tent of him who led
Their fathers into ambush. And through the house
The ghost must walk where none remembers his name,
And see nothing he knows in his childhood's room.

Age, then, blurs all; whose age it does not matter,
For any years will curl the ivy over
The windows behind which nothing happens yet,
And, even without the sun, the rain will fall
To write in walls a deepening signature,
While far from sight water grows in the well.
The mean becomes the cherished, if it remains.

A new age, perhaps, will change our cruelty
Into the quaint naughtiness of story,
Its dismal end always put off till to-morrow;
Someone may excuse the works we have reared,
Read charm in error, as an ancient fresco
Pardons the hand that fashioned it and murder;

Some ghost of ours may stop, and from his window
With dead eyes watch the death of the last gun,
The grasp of power as feeble as his own.

BEOWULF

So, bored with dragons, he lay down to sleep,
Locking for good his massive hoard of words
(Discuss and illustrate), forgetting now
The hope of heathens, muddled thoughts on fate.

Councils would have to get along without him:
The peerless prince had taken his last bribe
(*Lif is læne*); useless now the byrnie
Hard and hand-locked, fit for a baseball catcher.

Only with Grendel was he man-to-man;
Grendel's dam was his only sort of woman
(Weak conjugation). After they were gone
How could he stand the bench-din, the yelp-word?

Someone has told us this man was a hero.
Must we then reproduce his paradigms,
Trace out his rambling regress to his forbears
(An instance of Old English harking-back)?

LESSONS

How long, when hand of master is withdrawn,
Will hand of pupil move as if it stayed?
The books once closed, the classroom blind run
  down,
Who thinks of lessons now there is no need?

Docility, of feature or of mind,
Is glad to wither when the tongue is free;
Even if one phrase, one shared thought, remained,
Ten more will come and go by half-past four.

Therefore let all who teach discard this pride,
That anything is learnt except to please;
When fingers touch, or how love's names are said,
Like any lessons, change with time and place;

So here and now, with individual care,
This one sole way hand may be laid on hand,
Voice only with one voice may learn to cry,
And thus tongue lie with tongue, thus mind
  with mind.

But out of school, all ways the hand will move,
Forget the private hour, and touch the world;
The voice will bawl, slur the accent of love,
The tongue slop sweets, the mind lounge home
  expelled.

MASTERS

That horse whose rider fears to jump will fall,
Riflemen miss if orders sound unsure;
They only are secure who seem secure;
    Who lose their voice, lose all.

Those whom heredity or guns have made
Masters, must show it by a common speech;
Expected words in the same tone from each
    Will always be obeyed.

Likewise with stance, with gestures, and with face;
No more than mouth need move when words are said,
No more than hand to strike, or point ahead;
    Like slaves, limbs learn their place.

In triumph as in mutiny unmoved,
These make their public act their private good,
Their words in lounge or courtroom understood,
    But themselves never loved.

The eyes that will not look, the twitching cheek,
The hands that sketch what mouth would fear to own,
Only these make us known, and we are known
    Only as we are weak:

By yielding mastery the will is freed,
For it is by surrender that we live,
And we are taken if we wish to give,
Are needed if we need.

THE LAST WAR

The first country to die was normal in the evening,
Ate a good but plain dinner, chatted with some friends
Over a glass, and went to bed soon after ten;
And in the morning was found disfigured and dead.
        That was a lucky one.

At breakfast the others heard about it, and kept
Their eyes on their plates. Who was guilty? No one
                knew,
But by lunch-time three more would never eat again.
The rest appealed for frankness, quietly cocked their
                guns,
        Declared "This can't go on".

They were right. Only the strongest turned up for tea:
The old ones with the big estates hadn't survived
The slobbering blindfold violence of the afternoon.
One killer or many? Was it a gang, or all-against-all?
        Somebody must have known.

But each of them sat there watching the others, until
Night came and found them anxious to get it over.
Then the lights went out. A few might have lived, even
                then;
Innocent, they thought (at first) it still mattered what
        You had or hadn't done.

They were wrong. One had been lenient with his
          servants;
Another ran an island brothel, but rarely left it;
The third owned a museum, the fourth a remarkable
          gun;
The name of a fifth was quite unknown, but in the end
          What was the difference? None.

Homicide, pacifist, crusader, cynic, gentile, jew
Staggered about moaning, shooting into the dark.
Next day, to tidy up as usual, the sun came in
When they and their ammunition were all used up,
          And found himself alone.

Upset, he looked them over, to separate, if he could, •
The assassins from the victims, but every face
Had taken on the flat anonymity of pain;
And soon they'll all smell alike, he thought, and
          felt sick,
          And went to bed at noon.

DIRTY STORY

Twice daily, at noon and dusk, if we are lucky,
We hear fresh news of you, an oral cutting
From your unlimited biography.

To-day a butcher, you cuckolded the grocer,
Fouling his sugar, in thirty seconds only,
All the while tickling a pretty customer;

Yesterday you posed as a winking parson
Or a gull from the north, cloaking your belly-laughter
With a false voice that mourned for what you'd done;

To-morrow, in what shrines gaily excreting,
Will you, our champion even if defeated,
Bring down a solemn edifice with one swing?

Hero of single action, epic expert,
Beggar prince and bandit chief of the sexy,
Spry Juan, lifter of the lifted skirt,

What is the secret of your howling successes—
Your tongue never tardy with the punch sentence,
Your you-know-what in fabulous readiness?

Is it no more than the researcher's patience
To ransack life's laboratory, and labour
Ten years distilling salts to be used once;

To nose out the precisely suitable landscape,
The curiously jealous, the uniquely randy,
Then blow them all up in a retort or rape?

If so, your exploits should be read in silence,
Words bred of such travail move none to smiling,
But all to an uneasy reverence:

Reverence at such will to live in stories;
Uneasy, because we see behind your glories
Our own nasty defeats, nastier victories.

THE REAL EARTH

She smiled when, put to bed at twilight,
  She saw the quilt prepare for night;
Guarding the sheep of fluff that lay
  In channelled fields, sewn squares by day,
She paced her pillow's neighbourhood,
  Its lace a frozen wood.

Grown up, she thought the earth a cover
  To pull up to the chin; to her
All scenes were blankets for her bed,
  Homely with warmth; all roads that led
Through rumpled fields to any town
  Seams on an eiderdown.

In her great bed one night, she trembled,
  And thought what covered her seemed cold,
Every moment more like the ground.
  Too drowsy now for fear, she found
Softly upflowing from her feet
  An unaired, a soiled sheet.

ALTERNATIVES

It starts: a white girl in a dark house
Alone with the piano, playing a short song;
Lilies and silk stand quiet, silent the street,
The oil-lamp void of flame. Her long dress
Is rigid at the hem when her arms move
To hush, not urge, the current of the notes.

Below in a red light stoops the murderer,
Black in the cellar among straw and glass.
Dust cracks under his feet, his finger scrapes
The limed wall, then the bottom stair's edge,
And soon the wooden door creaks and yawns;
He shuffles towards the music. It ends.

Let bewilderment tie his hands, I cry,
Some flower in the wallpaper bind his brain,
So that the girl's room never fills with him
And the song never ends, I never hear
The jangling as her body falls awry
And the black lid shuts on her clenched hands.

But something says: Neither or both for you;
The house always empty, or this end.
Or would you rather she smiled as she played,
Hearing a step she knows, and sitting still,
Waited for the hands to move, not round
Her throat, but to her eager breasts?

WRONG WORDS

Half-shut, our eye dawdles down the page
Seeing the word love, the word death, the word life,
Rhyme-words of poets in a silver age:
Silver of the bauble, not of the knife.

Too fluent, drenching with confectionery
One image, one event's hard outline,
The words of failure's voluptuary
Descant around love—love of a routine.

There follow high words from a thwarted child
Rightly denied what it would foul, threatening
Grown-ups with its death, eager to gild
The pose of writhing with the pose of resigning.

But loneliness, the word never said,
Pleads to be recognised through their conceits;
Behind their frantic distortion lies the dread,
Unforced, unblurred, of real defeats:

Their real ladies would not follow the book,
Wrong ladies, happy with wrong words, wrong lives;
Careening now, they blazed, while none would look,
The distress signals of their superlatives.

A DREAM OF FAIR WOMEN

The door still swinging to, and girls revive,
Aeronauts in the utmost altitudes
    Of boredom fainting, dive
Into the bright oxygen of my nod;
Angels as well, a squadron of draped nudes,
    They roar towards their god.

Militant all, they fight to take my hat,
No more as yet; the other men retire
    Insulted, gestured at;
Each girl presses on me her share of what
Makes up the barn-door target of desire:
    And I am a crack shot.

Speech fails them, amorous, but each one's look,
Endorsed in other ways, begs me to sign
    Her body's autograph-book;
"Me first, Kingsley; I'm cleverest" each declares,
But no gourmet races downstairs to dine,
    Nor will I race upstairs.

Feigning aplomb, perhaps for half an hour,
I hover, and am shown by each princess
    The entrance to her tower;
Open, in that its tenant throws the key
At once to anyone, but not unless
    The anyone is me.

25

Now from the corridor their fathers cheer,
Their brothers, their young men; the cheers
    increase
  As soon as I appear;
From each I win a handshake and sincere
Congratulations; from the chief of police
  A nod, a wink, a leer.

This over, all delay is over too;
The first eight girls (the roster now agreed)
  Leap on me, and undo . . .
But honesty impels me to confess
That this is "all a dream", which was, indeed,
  Not difficult to guess.

But wait; not "just a dream", because, though
    good
And beautiful, it is also true, and hence
  Is rarely understood;
Who would choose any feasible ideal
In here and now's giant circumference,
  If that small room were real?

Only the best; the others find, have found
Love's ordinary distances too great,
  And, eager, stand their ground;
Map-drunk explorers, dry-land sailors, they
See no arrival that can compensate
  For boredom on the way;

26

And, seeming doctrinaire, but really weak,
Limelighted dolls guttering in their brain,
  They come with me, to seek
The halls of theoretical delight,
The women of that ever-fresh terrain,
  The night after to-night.

THE SILENT ROOM

In his low-ceilinged oaken room
The corpse finds pastimes of the tomb
  Cramped into scratching nose
  And counting fingers, toes.

Soon tiring of one-man charades,
He longs for books, a wireless, cards,
  Anything that might keep
  His dusty eyes from sleep.

For sleep would bring too-accurate
Dreams of the heavenly garden-fête
  Where the immortals walk,
  Pledged to immortal talk.

Dazed by respect or laughter, he
Would reel from saw to repartee,
  Ecstatic for the first
  Five thousand hours, at worst.

Verbal set-pieces yet would blaze,
And rocket-patterns yet amaze
  For twice as long, to draw
  His eye, not now his awe;

Then to one glow the varied fire
Would sink, the breezy bangs expire

In mutters, and the bare
Sticks char in the bright air.

The walkers on the endless lawn
Talk but to hide an endless yawn,
    Stale in the mouth of each
    An old, unwanted speech.

Foreseeing then a second sleep
(Of unknown dreams), the corpse must keep
    Permanently awake,
    And wait for an earthquake.

Earthquakes are few, brief their effect.
But wood soon rots: he can expect
    A far less rare relief
    From boredom, and less brief;

At last, maddened but merry, he
Finds never-tiring company:
    Slug, with foul rhymes to tell;
    Worm, with small-talk from hell.

AGAINST ROMANTICISM

A traveller who walks a temperate zone
  —Woods devoid of beasts, roads that please
      the foot—
Finds that its decent surface grows too thin:
  Something unperceived fumbles at his nerves.
To please an ingrown taste for anarchy
  Torrid images circle in the wood,
And sweat for recognition up the road,
  Cramming close the air with their bookish cries.
All senses then are glad to gasp: the eye
  Smeared with garish paints, tickled up with
      ghosts
That brandish warnings or an abstract noun;
  Melodies from shards, memories from coal,
Or saws from powdered tombstones thump the ear;
  Bodies rich with heat wriggle to the touch,
And verbal scents made real spellbind the nose;
  Incense, frankincense; legendary the taste
Of drinks or fruits or tongues laid on the tongue.
  Over all, a grand meaning fills the scene,
And sets the brain raging with prophecy,
  Raging to discard real time and place,
Raging to build a better time and place
  Than the ones which give prophecy its field
To work, the calm material for its rage,
  And the context which makes its prophecy.

Better, of course, if images were plain,
　　Warnings clearly said, shapes put down quite
　　　　still
Within the fingers' reach, or else nowhere;
　　But complexities crowd the simplest thing,
And flaw the surface that they cannot break.
　　Let us make at least visions that we need:
Let mine be pallid, so that it cannot
　　Force a single glance, form a single word;
An afternoon long-drawn and silent, with
　　Buildings free from all grime of history,
The people total strangers, the grass cut,
　　Not long, voluble swooning wilderness,
And green, not parched or soured by frantic suns
　　Doubling the commands of a rout of gods,
Nor trampled by the havering unicorn;
　　Let the sky be clean of officious birds
Punctiliously flying on the left;
　　Let there be a path leading out of sight,
And at its other end a temperate zone:
　　Woods devoid of beasts, roads that please
　　　　the foot.

DEPARTURE

For one month afterwards the eye stays true,
And sees the other's face held still and free
Of ornament; then tires of peering down
A narrow vista, and the month runs out.

Too young, this eye will claim the merit of
A faithful sentry frozen at his post
And not a movement seen; yet ranges over
Far other tracts, its object lost, corrupt.

Nor should I now swell to halloo the names
Of feelings that no one needs to remember,
Nor caper with my posy of wilted avowals
To clutter up your path I should wish clear.

Perhaps it is not too late to crane the eye
And find you, distant and small, but as you are;
If not, I will retain you honestly blurred,
Not a bland refraction of sweet mirrors.

SWANSEA BAY

Maps look impressive; to be anywhere
In villages rich with conventional signs,
Knowing that things ten miles away are there,
Seems happiness; roads fenced by dotted lines
Must run between pictorial solitudes;
Waters deserve their blue of remote, still,
And best at evening; and enamelled green
Becomes a phrase again, furnishing woods
With billiard-table moss, baize-apron leaves.
All must run for once to our own will,
Be and enact our need, and none believes
That any sour notes hide in a scored scene.

The far side of this bay is like a map:
Something small denotes a tower, a steeple,
Shading points out the contoured slopes, a scrap
Of smoke is houses, and movement movement of people.
They are the chance effect, the frontal mess
Against the background's paper authority;
However trite, some kind of recognition
—Immodesties of love or weariness—
Has got to make their presence relevance,
To see in a blank field an absent city;
People must enter the eye's lonely dance,
Or leave it reeling at its blind vision.

ON STAYING STILL

Half-way down the beach
A broken boat lies;
Black in every light,
But squeezed by sand that glows
From black to chocolate
Then ginger-dust. The seas
Soak it for no reason
Each tide-rise, finding it
Dried by the sun for no
Reason, or already wet
With rain before they are near
To strike poses of passion:
Bravery of blind colour,
Noble gesture of spray,
And eloquence of loud noise
That shake not a single spar.
The hulk's only use
Is as mark for pebble-thrower
Or shade for small anemone,
But that is not nothing;
And staying still is more,
When all else is moving
To no end, whether
Or not choice is free.
Good that decay recalls

(By being slow and steady)
Blossom, fruitful change
Of tree to coal, not any
Changeless tidal fury.

NERVES

The sun sinks behind houses, much too early;
Its warmth leaves stone and flesh, and the body
   Drowses, and safe in the dark
The nerves creep out, much too quickly.

They breed heat, no warmth, by their own writhing;
Their tremor is the tremor of the unwilling
   Hand, which to steady itself
Must touch somebody or something.

They twitch the head down in mock approval,
Mock humility, mock self-acquittal;
   They make the will an ant
Scuttling about its chalked circle.

For outlet, give me a fourth dimension;
For health, seal off this moist possession
   Behind sterilised flesh;
Sear it with a vast midday's iron,

Before some winter solstice lets it run
Through the small day to build its furred cocoon
   From head to foot, unbroken
Between me and air, movement, the sun.

THE END

The mirror holds: small common objects fill
Its eye impatient, sore with keeping still.
    The book, the person stupefy,
    Merely because they fill its eye.

The mirror breaks, and fragments wheel and flare
—Before their mercury dissolves in air—
    To seize the person for one look,
    To catch one image of the book.

THE VALUE OF SUFFERING

Surrounded for years with all the most assured
Tokens of size and sense—the broad thick table
Triple-banked with food, too much to eat, and
　　flowers
Too mixed and many to smell, and ladies too
Ready, sating ambition before it formed—
He went on hunting in the right costume,
Postured among the stolid falconers
(But lobbed his purses to the lutanists),
And, as the eldest son, was first in all
Exercises of eye, mouth, hand and loins.

Then mildew broke across the azure hangings,
Mould on his leather; his horse declined to stir
For all he made it bleed, and his men had time
To jeer at him before the fire took them.
Now, shaven head abased, sandalled feet slow,
He roams the crumbled courts and speaks to none;
But all crave blessing from his hand that clasps
A book, who never feared its pretty sword.

What a shame that a regal house must founder,
Its menials die, its favourites undergo
Unheard-of rape, to emphasise a contrast,
To point one thing out to one person;
Especially since the person could have seen

What it was all about by watching faces
After his father's joke, instead of laughing,
By changing places with his groom,
   By sixty seconds' thought.

THE SOURCES OF THE PAST

A broken flower-stem, a broken vase,
  A matchbox torn in two and thrown
Among the scraps of glass:
  At a last meeting, these alone
Record its ruptures, bound its violence,
  And make a specious promise to retain
This charted look of permanence
  In the first moment's pain.

But now the door slams, the steps retreat;
  Into one softness night will blur
The diverse, the hard street;
  And memory will soon prefer
That polished set of symbols, glass and rose
  (By slight revision), to the real mess
Of stumbling, arguing, yells, blows:
  To real distress.

All fragments of the past, near and far,
  Come down to us framed in a calm
No contemplations jar;
  But they grub it up from lapse of time,
And, could we strip that bland order away,
  What vulgar agitation would be shown:
What aimless hauntings behind clay,
  What fussing behind stone?

THE TRIUMPH OF LIFE

When Uncle Pandar Drink pulls down the blinds,
All sequence falters: life, the moving reel,
No longer smoothly, constantly unwinds,

But jerks from still to still. So, we reveal
(Watching no others' poses but our own)
What sober alcohols make us conceal;

Not what we show, but that it shall be shown,
Is all we care about at this first stage,
And that's the time to leave the stuff alone.

Later, we pose with purpose, try to gauge
The look of halted bodies, faces, eyes,
Scissored and pasted on our album-page.

Robbed of its cause and motive, nothing dies.
The darling moment, asked like this, will stay.
—Some time the cogs must mesh, we realise,

The figures move again. But what they say
And how they look no longer matters much:
People get up and dress and go away,

But photographs will never leave our touch.

THE TRIUMPH OF TIME

When Party-Member Lech lifts up his knout,
We know that's funny and unfunny;
When he gives you a clout,

That's funny, your friends agree,
But for you the joke falls flat.
(Now love's different, do you see.)

We can, we must, we will put up with that:
A man can't go on laughing all the time,
Or minding being laughed at,

And, far from being mere slime or grime,
This is the origin, I propound,
Of our ideas concerning the sublime.

That's fair; but will it still be, when we're found
Fustily grinning at a leg-show,
Funny and unfunny the other way round?

HERE IS WHERE

Here, where the ragged water
Is twilled and spun over
Pebbles backed like beetles,
Bright as beer-bottles
Bits of it like snow beaten,
Or milk boiling in saucepan ...

Going well so far, eh?
But soon, I'm sorry to say,
The here-where recipe
Will have to intrude its *I*,
Its main verb *want*,
Its *this* at some tangent.

What has this subject
Got to do with that object?
Why drag in
All that water and stone?
Scream the place down *here*,
There's nobody *there*.

The country, to townies,
Is hardly more than nice,
A window-box, pretty
When the afternoon's empty;
When a visitor waits,
The window shuts.

THE TWO PURSES

A satin purse, devoutly lined
With silk shot many ways, and crammed
Full of mirror, pencil, puff,
Its outside monogrammed,
Within as personally signed
By paper money, smooth and smart:

Such at least would be gift enough,
Device of a rich heart;
—These coins, worn thin, of dull
Metal, this purse of slack wool:
Can you use up this gift of love
And yet find it as durable?

NOCTURNE

Under the winter street-lamps, near the bus-stop,
Two people with nowhere to go fondle each other,
Writhe slowly in the entrance to a shop.
In the intervals of watching them, a sailor
Yaws about with an empty beer-flagon,
Looking for something good to smash it on.

Mere animals: on this the Watch Committee
And myself seem likely to agree;
But all this fumbling about, this wasteful
Voiding of sweat and breath—is that *animal*?

Nothing so sure and economical.

These keep the image of another creature
In crippled versions, cocky, drab and stewed;
What beast holds off its paw to gesture,
Or gropes towards being understood?

ACT OF KINDNESS

To really give the really valuable,
Or offer the last cigarette,
When shops are shut, to the ungrateful,
Or praise our betters—wishing, we forget

That anything we own is nearly cash,
And to have less of it is dead loss,
That unshared cigarettes are smoke and ash,
That praise is gross.

Not giving should be not living; how to live,
How to deal with any wish to give
When the gift gets stuck to the fingers?
We give nothing we have,
So smiling at strangers

Best suits our book—they cannot tell
Our own from others' words; generous
With common property we seem amiable;
Not to draw a knife
Looks like an act of kindness,
And is, acted to the life.

AIMING AT A MILLION

And one sort is always trying
To be champion darling,
Bush giant, forest king.

Assorted dryads, gentle,
Raving or doped, shall straddle
That god-almighty bole.

It can no more be the biggest
Than one leaf in a forest
Can dwarf or dry the rest,

And the biggest beauty
Is almost ugly,
Is, or soon will be,

Fleshy and animal,
Or hard and metal.
Then should it stay small?

None outgrows dying,
But height is the end of growing.
A lot is better than nothing.

FAIR SHARES FOR ALL

A nude steak posing behind gauze
Wins only gastropaths' applause.

An appetite that can be teased
Must be an appetite diseased.

This diagnosis may have point
When love's delivered with the joint.

TO EROS

If only we could throw you away,
Garotte you, weight you, sink you in the bay,
  We could start living, we say.

  Our girls would all relapse
Back into girls—not all that bright, perhaps,
  But ever such decent chaps,

  And when we took them out
To the Sea View, "Doris" we'd hear them shout,
  "Six pints, please, and a milk stout."

  Should we have the sense to go on
Our labour chief, our thick-lipped roarer gone?
  Or should we re-enter upon

  That boring welter of blue,
And at last clear off, not to get shot of you,
  As heroes used to do,

  But parching, fed at the oars,
To nab some hodge with bum and scruff like yours
  And bundle him to these shores?

ALBUM-LEAF

A photograph can't speak or move its face,
And so the ones we find in frames and books
Seem like the real faces of you and me
Now we no longer like each other's looks;
Self-regard cramps them to stupidity;
Their history of movement leaves no trace.

And this is scarcely queer, but it was queer
That once, during a well-composed embrace,
Something disturbed that studio veneer;
The self-regard of each got holed right through,
Or else we wished it had, or seemed to.

ODE TO THE
EAST-NORTH-EAST-BY-EAST WIND

You rush to greet me at the corner like
　　A cheery chap I can't avoid,
And blow my hair into one leaning spike
　　To show you're never unemployed.
You sweating, empty-handed labourer,
You bloody-rowelled, mailless courier,
　　Before you rush off somewhere new,
　　　　Just tell us what you do.

We know, of course, you blow the windmills round,
　　And that's a splendid thing to do;
Sometimes you pump up water from the ground;
　　Why, darling, that's just fine of you!
And round Mount Everest—such fun!—you blow
Gigantic bits of rock about, for no
　　Reason—but every little boy
　　　　Must have his little toy.

The old map-makers must have known you well
　　(Punch-drunk sea-captains put them wise)
To draw you with an infant's cheeks that swell
　　So that they shut your puffy eyes;
No need for you to care or notice where
You kick and writhe and scream in wincing air,
　　Telling the void of your distress,
　　　　Raving at emptiness.

51

Well now, since blowing things apart's your scheme,
    The crying child your metaphor,
Poetic egotists make you their theme,
    Finding in you their hatred for
A world that will not mirror their desire.
Silly yourself, you flatter and inspire
    Some of the silliest of us.
      And is that worth the fuss?

A POET'S EPITAPH

They call you "drunk with words"; but when we drink
And fetch it up, we sluice it down the sink.
You should have stuck to spewing beer, not ink.

Between the GARDENING and the COOKERY
    Comes the brief POETRY shelf;
By the Nonesuch Donne, a thin anthology
    Offers itself.

Critical, and with nothing else to do,
    I scan the Contents page,
Relieved to find the names are mostly new;
    No one my age.

Like all strangers, they divide by sex:
    Landscape near Parma
Interests a man, so does *The Double Vortex*,
    So does *Rilke and Buddha*.

"I travel, you see", "I think" and "I can read"
    These titles seem to say;
But *I Remember You, Love is my Creed,*
    Poem for J.,

The ladies' choice, discountenance my patter
    For several seconds;
From somewhere in this (as in any) matter
    A moral beckons.

Should poets bicycle-pump the human heart
    Or squash it flat?

54

Man's love is of man's life a thing apart;
    Girls aren't like that.

We men have got love well weighed up; our stuff
    Can get by without it.
Women don't seem to think that's good enough;
    They write about it,

And the awful way their poems lay them open
    Just doesn't strike them.
Women are really much nicer than men:
    No wonder we like them.

Deciding this, we can forget those times
    We sat up half the night
Chockfull of love, crammed with bright thoughts,
        names, rhymes,
    And couldn't write.

CREEPER

Shaving this morning, I look out of the
  window
In expectation: will another small
Tendril of ivy, dry and straw-yellow,
Have put its thin clasp on the garden wall?

Oh dear no. A few arid strands, a few
Curled-up leaves, are all that's left of it.
The children pulled it up for something to do.
My mouth sets in its usual post-box slit.

Fled is that vision of a bottle-green
Fur-coat of foliage muffling the pale brick,
Stamping into the flat suburban scene
A proof of beauty, lovable exotic.

Of course, I know ivy will sweetly plump
Itself all over, shyly barge into crannies,
Pull down lump after elegiac lump,
Then tastefully screen ruin from our eyes.

Then it would all become a legal quibble:
Whose what has wrecked what how and by
  whose what;
And moral: is turning stout wall to rubble
A fool's trick in fact, but not in thought?

We should be thankful to be spared all that
When bank-clerk longings get a short answer,
When someone snatches off our silly hat
And drop-kicks it under a steamroller.

GULLS

A dozen gulls from the seashore
Across the road swim on a pool
Of rain spilt on the meadow's floor,

And, being off-white, rearrange
Meadow as barnyard, pool as pond,
Themselves as ducks; and this exchange

At first seems meant to entertain,
Merely to fool, or criticise
The sort to whom rain must be rain,

Gulls gulls; or is this hinted at:
No fake is fake—there is no *this*
Less this just for not being *that*?

A PILL FOR THE IMPRESSIONABLE

Derelict sheds seen from the train,
Standing for nothing in the rain,
Walls lying prone in heaps of stone,

Cold hearths where weeds can barely live,
Quote to the passing sensitive
Banal and clear: *Something died here.*

And something dead invites his tears
Until, miles later, there appears
A graveyard scene in white and green.

In contrast, this looks quite all right;
Smooth turf, rolled paths, well-chosen site:
Everything there in good repair.

If deserts are a larger death,
Why should the traveller catch his breath
When the old ticker gives a kick?

London could die beside the track
To palliate this heart-attack.
The tears we feign are inhumane.

THEY ONLY MOVE

They only move who travel far,
So whisk me off down roads unsigned
And take me where the good times are.

Whizz past the dance-hall and the bar;
All muffled contact must be blind.
They only move who travel far.

Bortsch, pâté, filthy caviare,
Say I've respectfully declined,
And take me where the good times are.

The social round—Martell, cigar,
Talk about talk—is social grind;
They only move who travel far.

Install me dozing in the car,
Wined, dined, but still unconcubined,
And take me where the good times are.

Lush pastures of the cinema
Will be demanded, once defined.
They only move who travel far.

Fear-indigestion, guilt-catarrh—
If these exist, leave them behind
And take me where the good times are.

Tell me, will movement make or mar?
Then root my body, tell my mind
They only move, who travel far
And take me where the good times are.

A NOTE ON WYATT

See her come bearing down, a tidy craft!
Gaily her topsails bulge, her sidelights burn!
There's jigging in her rigging fore and aft,
And beauty's self, not name, limned on her stern.

See at her head the Jolly Roger flutters!
"God, is she fully manned? If she's one short..."
Cadet, bargee, longshoreman, shellback mutters;
Drowned is reason that should me comfort.

But habit, like a cork, rides the dark flood,
And, like a cork, keeps her in walls of glass;
Faint legacies of brine tingle my blood,
The tide-wind's fading echoes, as I pass.

Now, jolly ship, sign on a jolly crew:
God bless you, dear, and all who sail in you.

THE GARDEN

Snuffing the scented afterglow
In summer gardens years ago,
   We tried to conjure there
   A person out of air.

Memory, mixing near with far,
Fiddles connections where none are:
   Perhaps, we now contrive,
   A person did arrive.

Bearings on moving points are bound
To give no sequence but a round;
   We measure and collate,
   But cannot put it straight,

And guzzle roses at the hour
That might have held that cryptic power,
   Half-asking what it meant,
   Half-granting half-assent.

Wanting to yield, yet just too old,
And just too young quite to withhold,
   We bag the middle way:
   You ask me first, we say.

From thinned or trembling lips we hear
Only what makes us wince or sneer:
 Yes, the response inane,
 Or *No*, the inhumane.

Debunking what our hearts adore,
Rebunking what our brains abhor,
 Indoors we now adjourn.
 Inward at last we turn.

Our mirror shows one loving face
Pleased to inhabit a blank space.
 To plead *I'm all alone*
 We should be on our own.

THE VOICE OF AUTHORITY:
A LANGUAGE GAME

Do this. Don't move. O'Grady says do this,
You get a move on, see, do what I say.
Look lively when I say O'Grady says.

Say this. Shut up. O'Grady says say this,
You talk fast without thinking what to say.
What goes is what I say O'Grady says.

Or rather let me put the point like this:
O'Grady says what goes is what I say
O'Grady says; that's what O'Grady says.

By substituting you can shorten this,
Since any god you like will do to say
The things you like, that's what O'Grady says.

The harm lies not in that, but in that this
Progression's first and last terms are I say
O'Grady says, not just O'Grady says.

Yet it's O'Grady must be out of this
Before what we say goes, not what we say
O'Grady says. Or so O'Grady says.

MIGHTIER THAN THE PEN

Jerking and twitching as he walks,
Neighing and hooting as he talks,
The shabby pundit's prototype,
Smoking his horrible black pipe,
Balbus keeps making me feel ill.
I've heard that art's a kind of pill
To purge your feelings, so I'll try
And catch him in my camera's eye,
Transcribe him down to the last hair,
Ambered, though neither rich nor rare.

But will my interests be served
By having such a sod preserved?
Is art much better than a drug,
To cure the man but spare the bug?
And, gentle reader, why should you
Be led vicariously to spew?
Cameras just click, and a click's not
The sound of an effective shot;
Fussing with flash and tripod's fun,
But bang's the way to get things done.

AUTOBIOGRAPHICAL FRAGMENT

When I lived down in Devonshire
  The callers at my cottage
Were Constant Angst, the art critic,
  And old Major Courage.

Angst always brought me something nice
  To get in my good graces:
A quilt, a roll of cotton-wool,
  A pair of dark glasses.

He tore up all my unpaid bills,
  Went and got my slippers,
Took the telephone off its hook
  And bolted up the shutters.

We smoked and chatted by the fire,
  Sometimes just nodding;
His charming presence made it right
  To sit and do nothing.

But then—those awful afternoons
  I walked out with the Major!
I ran up hills, down streams, through briars;
  It was sheer blue murder.

Trim in his boots, riding-breeches
    And threadbare Norfolk jacket,
He watched me, frowning, bawled commands
    To work hard and enjoy it.

I asked him once why I was there,
    Except to get all dirty;
He tugged his grey moustache and snapped:
    "Young man, it's your duty."

What duty's served by pointless, mad
    Climbing and crawling?
I tell you, I was thankful when
    The old bore stopped calling.

A SONG OF EXPERIENCE

A quiet start: the tavern, our small party,
    A dark-eyed traveller drinking on his own;
We asked him over when the talk turned hearty,
    And let him tell of women he had known.

He tried all colours, white and black and coffee;
    Though quite a few were chary, more were bold;
Some took it like the host, some like a toffee;
    The two or three who wept were soon consoled.

For seven long years his fancies were tormented
    By one he often wheedled, but in vain;
At last, oh Christ in heaven, she consented,
    And the next day he journeyed on again.

The inaccessible he laid a hand on,
    The heated he refreshed, the cold he warmed.
What Blake presaged, what Lawrence took a stand on,
    What Yeats locked up in fable, he performed.

And so he knew, where we can only fumble,
    Wildly in daydreams, vulgarly in art;
Miles past the point where all delusions crumble
    He found the female and the human heart.

69

Then love was velvet on a hand of iron
  That wrenched the panting lover from his aim;
Lion rose up as lamb and lamb as lion,
  Nausicaa and Circe were the same.

What counter-images, what cold abstraction
  Could start to quench that living element,
The flash of prophecy, the glare of action?
  —He drained his liquor, paid his score and went.

I saw him, brisk in May, in Juliet's weather,
  Hitch up the trousers of his long-tailed suit,
Polish his windscreen with a chamois-leather,
  And stow his case of samples in the boot.

THE ENGLISH NOVEL, 1740–1820

The open road winds down from Wilson's farm
To neat lawns and a gilt-edged paradise
Where Pamela walks out on D'Arcy's arm,
And Fanny Goodwill bobs to Fanny Price.

ROMANCE

The sound of saxophones, like farmhouse cream,
Plus long skirts and fair heads in a soft gleam,
Both scale and are the forest-fence of dream.

Picture a youngster in the lonely night
Who finds a stepping-stone from dark to bright,
An undrawn curtain and an arm of light.

Here was an image nothing could dispel:
Adulthood's high romantic citadel,
The Tudor Ballroom of the Grand Hotel.

Those other dreams, those freedoms lost their charm,
Those twilight lakes reflecting pine or palm,
Those skies were merely large and wrongly calm.

What then but weakness turns the heart again
Out in that lonely night beyond the pane
With images and truths of wind and rain?